When You've Got To Go!

John Townsend & Carolyn Scrace

I've gotta go!

First published in the UK in 2020 by The Salariya Book Company Ltd
This edition published in the UK in 2025 by Hatch Press,
an imprint of Bonnier Books UK
4th Floor, Victoria House
Bloomsbury Square, London WC1B 4DA
Owned by Bonnier Books
Sveavägen 56, Stockholm, Sweden
www.bonnierbooks.co.uk

Copyright © 2025 by Hatch Press

1 3 5 7 9 10 8 6 4 2

All rights reserved

ISBN 978-1-83587-121-8

Edited by Rebecca Kealy
Production by Hannah Cartwright

Printed in China

Meet the Monster Squad!

Hello! My name is Zork.

Hi, I'm Curly.

My name is Rocky.

We're the friendly Monster Squad!

We scribble and we write,
making manners fun and cool,
to show you what is right.

RESPECT

Manners Matter

Thank you!

Some little children can forget
to leave clean rooms behind them.
So we're the friendly Monster Squad,
we're here to help remind them.

Oops!

If you need to use a potty, **make sure** you're quick, don't wait...
For if you stop to think or play, you might just be too late!

Have a make-sure before you go out!

Before you zoom off on your trip,
make sure you've tried to go.
So when the journey's started,
there's no need to stop or slow!

Vroom
Vroom

As soon as Zork was big enough,
he didn't need his potty.

I can use the toilet now,
and reach it with my botty!

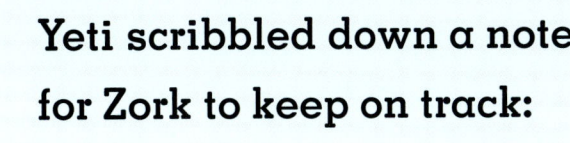
Yeti scribbled down a note for Zork to keep on track:

Always use the toilet roll and wipe from front to back.

Gently push and close the door;
you're in your private zone.
If someone needs the bathroom too,
they'll knock and make themselves known.

When Curly was much littler, he had a silly habit. Because he didn't like the flush — he never went to **grab it!**

Here's Rocky with some good advice from when things once went wrong:

I went outside to play for hours and left it far too long...

The toilet felt too far from me

and I was deep in play.

And so a little accident

upset my happy day!

Yeti gives some good advice
When Zork gets in a muddle...
He sometimes doesn't aim too well,
And leaves a little puddle.

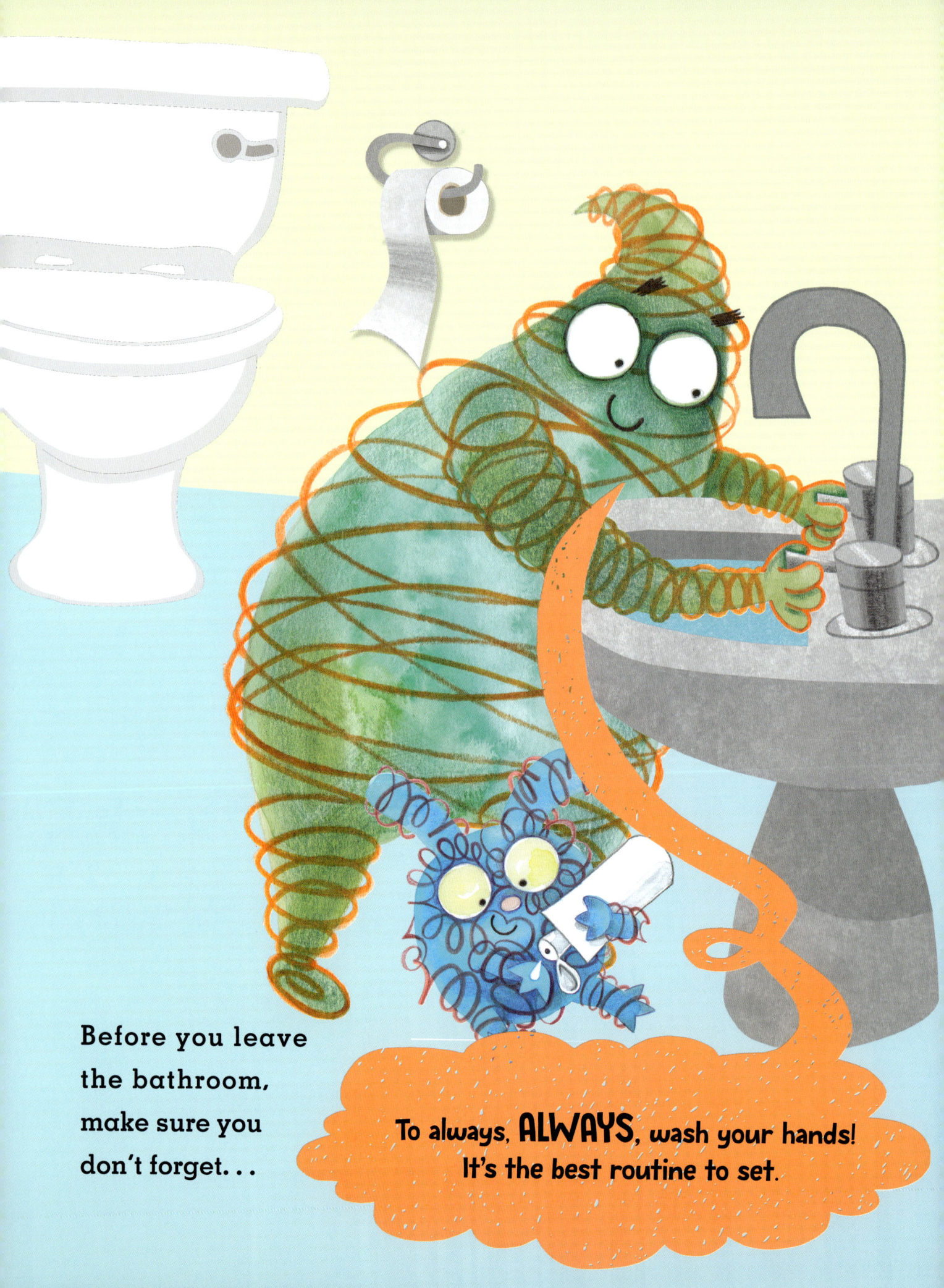

Before you leave the bathroom, make sure you don't forget...

To always, ALWAYS, wash your hands! It's the best routine to set.

HAVE YOU HEARD THE MAGIC WORDS?

Don't be grotty with a potty

The Monster Squad now wave goodbye
with friendly flags and banners,
to help us all remember well,
our new toilet-time manners!

When you've been, please leave it clean

CAN YOU HELP US FIND THE ANSWERS TO THIS QUIZ?

QUESTION 1

When I'm on the potty, should I sit still or move around?

QUESTION 2

What is a **make-sure**?

MORE MONSTER QUESTIONS

QUESTION 5

When we're done, what should we do to the toilet?

QUESTION 6

When we need to use the potty, should we aim to the side?